READY,

STEADY,

PRACTISE!

Paul Broadbent

Mental Arithmetic
Pupil Book **Year 4**

Features of this book

- Clear explanations and worked examples for each mental arithmetic topic from the KS2 National Curriculum.

- Questions split into three sections that become progressively more challenging:

  Warm up

  Test yourself

  Challenge yourself

- 'How did you do?' checks at the end of each topic for self-evaluation.

- Regular progress tests to assess pupils' understanding and recap on their learning.

- Answers to every question in a pull-out section at the centre of the book.

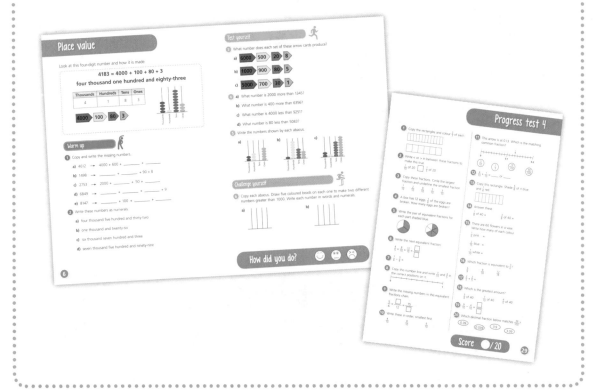

Contents

Counting and numbers

Counting patterns can use steps of different numbers.
To work out the steps, look at the difference between the numbers.

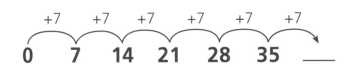

This is going up in multiples of seven. The next number is 42.

When you count backwards past zero you will use negative numbers. Picture them on a number line to help you see them in sequence.

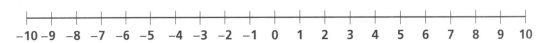

1 Copy each sequence and write the missing numbers.

a) 12   18   _____   30   _____   42   _____

b) _____   _____   100   125   150   _____   200

c) 27   _____   45   54   _____   _____   81

d) 7   14   21   _____   _____   _____   49

e) 2000   3000   _____   _____   _____   7000   8000

2 Write the next two numbers in each of these sequences.

a) 106   101   96   91   86

b) 71   74   77   80   83

c) 83   77   71   65   59

d) 230   280   330   380   430

e) 169   167   165   163   161

3 Write the number for each letter.

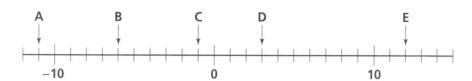

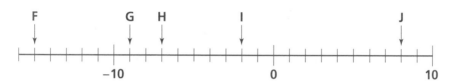

4 592 is the halfway number between 588 and 596.

588 ------ 592 ------ 596

What are the halfway numbers between these numbers?

a) 580 _____ 620

b) 945 _____ 961

c) 422 _____ 482

d) 678 _____ 700

Challenge yourself

5 Count in these steps. Write the three missing numbers for each.

a) Count in 10s → 972 _____ _____ _____ 1012

b) Count in 10s → 4000 _____ _____ _____ 4040

c) Count in 100s → 859 _____ _____ _____ 1259

d) Count in 100s → 6923 _____ _____ _____ 7323

e) Count in 1000s → 519 _____ _____ _____ 4519

f) Count in 1000s → 6795 _____ _____ _____ 10 795

How did you do?

Place value

Look at this four-digit number and how it is made.

4183 = 4000 + 100 + 80 + 3

four thousand one hundred and eighty-three

Thousands	Hundreds	Tens	Ones
4	1	8	3

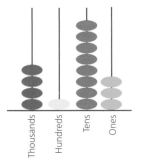

Warm up

1. Copy and write the missing numbers.

   a) 4612 ⟶ 4000 + 600 + _____ + _____

   b) 1498 ⟶ _____ + _____ + 90 + 8

   c) 2753 ⟶ 2000 + _____ + 50 + _____

   d) 6849 ⟶ _____ + _____ + _____ + 9

   e) 8147 ⟶ _____ + 100 + _____ + _____

2. Write these numbers as numerals.

   a) four thousand five hundred and thirty-two

   b) one thousand and twenty-six

   c) six thousand seven hundred and three

   d) seven thousand five hundred and ninety-nine

3 What number does each set of these arrow cards produce?

a)

6000 500 20 8

b)

1000 900 80 5

c)

5000 700 30 1

4 a) What number is 2000 more than 1345?

b) What number is 400 more than 6356?

c) What number is 4000 less than 9251?

d) What number is 80 less than 5083?

5 Write the numbers shown by each abacus.

a)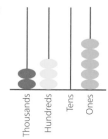

b)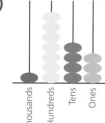

c)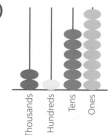

Challenge yourself

6 Copy each abacus. Draw five coloured beads on each one to make two different numbers greater than 1000. Write each number in words and numerals.

a)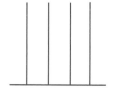

b)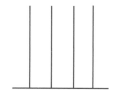

Comparing and ordering numbers

Remember that < and > are used to compare numbers.

1439 < 1827	**4503 > 4305**
< means 'is less than'	**> means 'is greater than'**
1439 is less than 1827	4503 is greater than 4305

When you compare numbers to put them in order, you must look carefully at the values of the digits.

If you have a list of four-digit numbers to put in order, look at the place value of the digits, starting with the thousands.

Example: Put these in order, starting with the smallest.

2345   4630   2092   2354   1785   ⟶   1785   2092   2345   2354   4630

Warm up

1) Copy and write < or > between the numbers to make these correct.

   a) 4065 ☐ 4550

   b) 5633 ☐ 5363

   c) 2703 ☐ 2699

   d) 4185 ☐ 4850

2) Look at this set of numbers. What is the smallest number? What is the largest number?

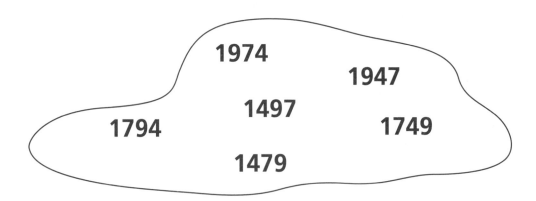

1974

1947

1497

1794

1749

1479

3 Write each set of numbers in order of size, starting with the smallest.

a)

3149	3150
2087	2900

b)

6102	5904
5933	6244

c)

8003	8030
8300	8303

d)

9213	8959
8599	9132

Challenge yourself

4 These are the heights of some of the tallest mountains around the world. Copy this table and write the mountains in height order starting with the tallest.

Aconcagua 6960 m

Chappal Waddi 2409 m

Cook 3766 m

Everest 8848 m

K2 8611 m

Kilimanjaro 5893 m

Lenin Peak 7134 m

McKinley 6194 m

Name of mountain	Height (m)

How did you do?

Addition

When doing addition with big numbers, break the numbers up so that you can add them in your head.

Example: What is 63 add 18?

63 + **18** =

63 + **10** + **8** =

73 + 8 =

70 + **3** + **8** = 70 + 11 = 81

Hold the bigger number in your head and break up the smaller number.

Example: Add together 273 and 40.

273 + 40 =

200 + **70** + **3** + 40 =

200 + **70** + 40 + **3** =

200 + 110 + 3 = 313

Add the hundreds and tens and then add on the ones.

Warm up

1 Add these mentally and write the answers.

a) 77 + 5 =

b) 58 + 9 =

c) 35 + 8 =

d) 86 + 7 =

e) 58 + 13 =

f) 47 + 25 =

g) 39 + 32 =

h) 68 + 19 =

2 Now add these mentally and write the answers.

a) 71 + 60 =

b) 64 + 50 =

c) 85 + 30 =

d) 68 + 40 =

e) 384 + 40 =

f) 257 + 60 =

g) 191 + 70 =

h) 239 + 80 =

3 Copy and complete these addition grids.

a)

+	80	60	90	70
253	333			
185				
693				

b)

+	45	38	52	127
35	80			
26				
241				

4 What are the missing digits 0–6 in these additions?

0   **2**   **4**   **6**

1   **3**   **5**

a) $45 + \boxed{}8 = 83$

b) $\boxed{}6 + 14 = 7\boxed{}$

c) $19 + 4\boxed{} = \boxed{}3$

d) $\boxed{}7 + 35 = 5\boxed{}$

Challenge yourself

5 I am thinking of a number. If I add 60 to my number, I end up with double the number I started with. What number was I thinking of?

How did you do?

Subtraction

There are different strategies you can use to subtract mentally.

Counting on from the smallest number is a good method.

> **Example: What is 45 subtract 18?**
>
> Count on from 18 to 20 and then to 45.
>
>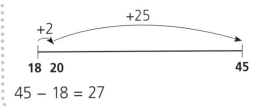
>
> $45 - 18 = 27$

You could try breaking numbers up so that you can subtract them in your head.

> **Example: Take away 80 from 135.**
>
> $$135 - 80 =$$
> $$130 + 5 - 80 =$$
> $$\underline{130 - 80 = 50} + 5 = 55$$
>
> Subtract the hundreds and tens and then add on the ones.

Warm up

1 Picture the jumps on these number lines to help you subtract these mentally.

a)
```
19                    56
```
$56 - 19 =$

b)
```
27                    43
```
$43 - 27 =$

c)
```
52                    91
```
$91 - 52 =$

d)
```
38                    85
```
$85 - 38 =$

e)
```
35                    64
```
$64 - 35 =$

f)
```
56                    74
```
$74 - 56 =$

2 Answer these calculations.

a) Take 60 away from 155.

b) Subtract 40 from 118.

c) What is 70 less than 142?

d) Take away 90 from 161.

e) What is 128 take away 50?

3 Copy and complete each chart with the numbers coming out of each subtraction machine.

a)

IN	155	163	105	132	111	149
OUT	85					

b)

IN	300	900	400	700	800	600
OUT	50					

Challenge yourself

4 Look at the heights of these sunflowers and answer these questions.

a) How many cm taller is Sunflower A than Sunflower B?

b) How many cm taller is Sunflower B than Sunflower C?

c) If Sunflower D grows to be the same height as Sunflower A, how many more centimetres will it need to grow?

d) What is the difference in height between Sunflower D and Sunflower E?

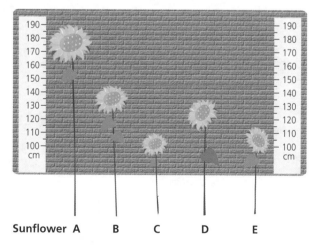

Sunflower A   B   C   D   E

e) How much shorter is Sunflower E than Sunflower B?

How did you do?

Progress test 1

1 Write the number each arrow points to.

2 What are the missing numbers?

5732 ⟶ 5000 + _____ + _____ + 2

3 Write the missing numbers in this sequence.

400   350   _____   _____   200

4 What number is 300 more than 1176?

5 Write the next two numbers in this sequence.

182   177   172

6 Write these numbers in order, starting with the smallest.

1956   1596   1965

7 Write the number shown on this abacus.

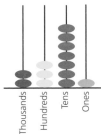

8 What is the halfway number?

380 _____ 440

9 Count in 10s and write the two missing numbers.

3430   _____   _____   3460

10 Copy these numbers. Underline the smallest number and circle the largest number.

6574   5674   5476   6745   7456

11 What is the halfway number?

218 _____ 242

12 Write the two numbers missing from this sequence.

28   _____   36   40   _____

13 Count in 100s and write the missing numbers.

882   _____   _____   1182

14 Write eight thousand nine hundred and fifteen in numerals.

15 Write the combined number.

8000 + 300 + 50 + 1 ⟶ _____

16 Which of the numbers below is 1000 more than 5701?

5801   6701   5711   6570

17 Write the number that each arrow points to.

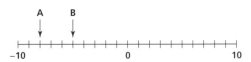

18 Write the next two numbers in this sequence.

88   92   96

19 Copy and write < or > in between these two sets of numbers to make these correct.

6060 ☐ 6006   5195 ☐ 5915

20 What number is 5000 less than 9470?

Score ⬤ / 20

1 150 − 70 =

2 What is the total of 26 and 35?

3 40 + _____ = 120

4 293 + 30 =

5 What number is 200 less than 818?

6 110 − _____ = 30

7 I am thinking of a number. If I subtract 60, I am left with 95. What is my number?

8 47 + 9 =

9 Subtract 150 from each of these numbers.

400

700

10 52 − 19 =

11 143 − 90 =

12 A jug holds 600 ml of milk and 250 ml is poured out. How much milk is left?

13 28 + 58 =

14 63 − 14 =

15 Add 30 to each of these numbers.

491

207

16 _____ − 70 = 56

17 53 + 28 =

18 In this addition wall the top number is the sum of the two numbers below. What is the missing number?

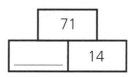

19 159 − _____ = 60

20 What number is 7 more than 55?

Multiplication and division facts

The 11 times table has an interesting pattern. Learn these facts.

11 × 1 = 11	11 × 5 = 55	11 × 9 = 99
11 × 2 = 22	11 × 6 = 66	11 × 10 = 110
11 × 3 = 33	11 × 7 = 77	11 × 11 = 121
11 × 4 = 44	11 × 8 = 88	11 × 12 = 132

The 12 times table is double the 6 times table.
You could also learn it by multiplying by 10 and then by 2.

Example:

12 × 7 ⟶ (10 × 7) + (2 × 7) = 84

12 × 1 = 12	12 × 5 = 60	12 × 9 = 108
12 × 2 = 24	12 × 6 = 72	12 × 10 = 120
12 × 3 = 36	12 × 7 = 84	12 × 11 = 132
12 × 4 = 48	12 × 8 = 96	12 × 12 = 144

Warm up

1. Write the two multiplication and two division facts for each set of numbers.

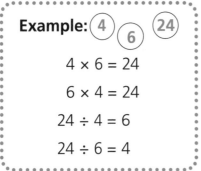

Example: (4) (6) (24)

4 × 6 = 24

6 × 4 = 24

24 ÷ 4 = 6

24 ÷ 6 = 4

a) (7) (35) (5)

b) (6) (7) (42)

c) (9) (4) (36)

d) (8) (6) (48)

e) (132) (11) (12)

f) (7) (63) (9)

16

2 In these multiplication triangles the top number is the product of the two numbers below. What are the missing numbers?

a)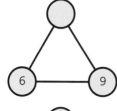

b)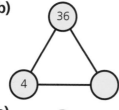

c)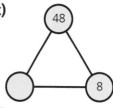

d)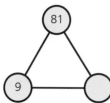

e)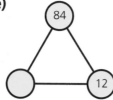

f)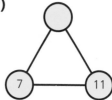

3 Use doubling to answer these.

a) $3 \times 3 =$

     $6 \times 3 =$

     $12 \times 3 =$

b) $3 \times 5 =$

     $6 \times 5 =$

     $12 \times 5 =$

c) $3 \times 8 =$

     $6 \times 8 =$

     $12 \times 8 =$

d) $3 \times 4 =$

     $6 \times 4 =$

     $12 \times 4 =$

e) $3 \times 9 =$

     $6 \times 9 =$

     $12 \times 9 =$

f) $3 \times 7 =$

     $6 \times 7 =$

     $12 \times 7 =$

4 Write the answers to these. Circle the answers you know instantly.

$8 \times 11 =$ $4 \times 7 =$ $3 \times 9 =$ $7 \times 6 =$

$12 \times 6 =$ $11 \times 2 =$ $9 \times 4 =$ $10 \times 8 =$

$7 \times 3 =$ $9 \times 2 =$ $6 \times 3 =$ $11 \times 11 =$

$5 \times 12 =$ $8 \times 7 =$ $9 \times 9 =$ $6 \times 8 =$

5 What's my number? Work out the mystery number for each of these.

a) When I divide my number by 7, the answer is 8.

b) When I multiply my number by 6, the answer is 42.

c) When I divide my number by 3 and then add 5, the answer is 12.

d) When I multiply my number by 5 and then subtract 6, the answer is 39.

How did you do? 🙂 😐 😣

Multiplication

Use the tables facts that you know to help you multiply bigger numbers.

$3 \times 5 = 15$

$300 \times 5 = 1500$

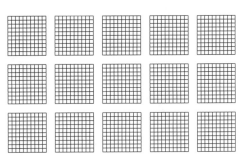

Try using factor pairs to help you multiply larger numbers.

Example: What is 35×8?

Break the numbers up into factor pairs:

5 and 7 are factors of 35   2 and 4 are factors of 8

$5 \times 7 \times 2 \times 4$ ← *Rearrange the factors to make them easier to multiply.*

$5 \times 2 \times 7 \times 4 = 10 \times 28$

So $35 \times 8 = 280$

Warm up

1 Answer these.

a) $4 \times 9 \ =$
     $400 \times 9 =$

b) $6 \times 8 \ =$
     $600 \times 8 =$

c) $8 \times 7 \ =$
     $800 \times 7 \ =$

d) $9 \times 3 \ =$
     $900 \times 3 =$

e) $7 \times 7 \ =$
     $700 \times 7 =$

f) $4 \times 12 \ =$
     $400 \times 12 =$

2 Copy and complete this multiplication grid.

×	30	60	80
20	600		
90			
40			

3 The two bottom numbers on each triangle are multiplied to give the top number. What are the missing numbers?

a)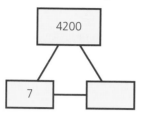

b)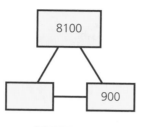

c)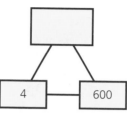

d)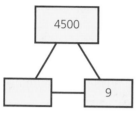

e)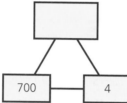

f)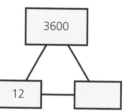

4 Multiply these sets of three numbers. Look for pairs to multiply first.

a)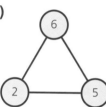

b)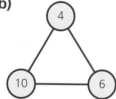

c)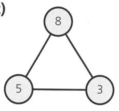

d)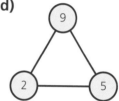

5 Write the factor pairs, then answer these multiplications.

a) **25 × 4**   Factors of 25: _____ _____   Factors of 4: _____ _____

_____ × _____ × _____ × _____ = _____

b) **15 × 8**   Factors of 15: —— ——   Factors of 8: _____ _____

_____ × _____ × _____ × _____ = _____

c) **35 × 6**   Factors of 35: _____ _____   Factors of 6: _____ _____

_____ × _____ × _____ × _____ = _____

d) **45 × 4**   Factors of 45: _____ _____   Factors of 4: _____ _____

_____ × _____ × _____ × _____ = _____

How did you do?

Division

When you divide large numbers, break the numbers up to help you work out division answers.

> **Example:** What is 54 divided by 3?
>
> Break 54 up into 30 and 24. $30 \div 3 = 10$
>
> $24 \div 3 = 8$
>
> So $54 \div 3 = 18$

Remember – if there are remainders in division problems, check that the answer makes sense. Should you round the answer up or down?

> **Example:** 15 pencils are shared equally between four people.
> **How many will each person get?**
>
> Three pencils each and three left over.
>
> **Example:** A box can hold four pencils.
> **How many boxes are needed for 15 pencils?**
>
> Four boxes, with one box of three pencils.

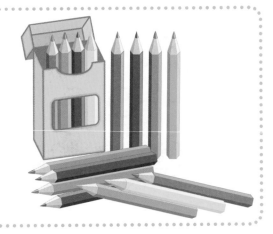

Warm up

1 Answer these divisions.

a) $60 \div 4 =$ b) $85 \div 5 =$

c) $57 \div 3 =$ d) $72 \div 6 =$

e) $91 \div 7 =$ f) $92 \div 4 =$

g) $78 \div 6 =$ h) $84 \div 3 =$

(2) Copy these divisions then write down the remainder for each division from the table.

61 ÷ 3

no remainder
1
2
3
4
5

84 ÷ 4

74 ÷ 6

92 ÷ 8

78 ÷ 5

86 ÷ 9

(3) Copy and complete each chart with the numbers coming out of each division machine.

a)  IN → ÷3 → OUT

IN	900	1500	2100	1200	2400	2700
OUT	300					

b)  IN → ÷4 → OUT

IN	800	2400	1200	3200	1600	2800
OUT	200					

(4) Mr Wilson sells all types of tyres. Answer these questions.

a) There are 49 bicycle tyres. How many bicycles can have a set of tyres?

b) There are 73 car tyres. How many cars can have four new tyres?

c) Buses have six wheels and Mr Wilson has 85 bus tyres. How many buses can have a full set of new tyres?

d) Mr Wilson stacks lorry tyres in piles of eight tyres.
How many full piles can he make with 45 tyres and how many tyres are left over?

How did you do?

Fractions

Remember that a fraction has two parts.

The **denominator** tells you the number of equal parts the whole is divided into.

The **numerator** tells you the number of those equal parts that are taken.

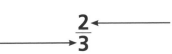

You can multiply or divide the denominator and numerator by the same number to make equivalent fractions.

This fraction strip shows some equivalent fractions.

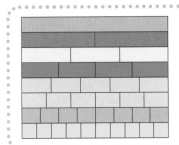

Example: Use the strip to show that $\frac{2}{3} = \frac{4}{6}$.

$$\frac{2}{3} = \frac{4}{6}$$

×2

×2

Warm up

1 Write the pairs of equivalent fractions shaded blue for each shape.

a)

b)

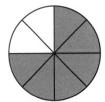

c)

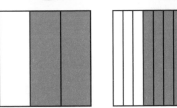

d)

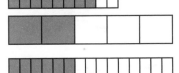

Answers

Pages 4–5
1. **a)** 24, 36, 48   **b)** 50, 75, 175
   c) 36, 63, 72   **d)** 28, 35, 42
   e) 4000, 5000, 6000
2. **a)** 81, 76   **b)** 86, 89   **c)** 53, 47
   d) 480, 530   **e)** 159, 157
3. −11, −6, −1, 3, 12
   −15, −9, −7, −2, 8
4. **a)** 600   **b)** 953   **c)** 452   **d)** 689
5. **a)** 982, 992, 1002   **b)** 4010, 4020, 4030
   c) 959, 1059, 1159   **d)** 7023, 7123, 7223
   e) 1519, 2519, 3519   **f)** 7795, 8795, 9795

Pages 6–7
1. **a)** 10, 2   **b)** 1000, 400
   c) 700, 3   **d)** 6000, 800, 40
   e) 8000, 40, 7
2. **a)** 4532   **b)** 1026   **c)** 6703   **d)** 7599
3. **a)** 6528   **b)** 1985   **c)** 5731
4. **a)** 3345   **b)** 6756   **c)** 5251   **d)** 5003
5. **a)** 2305   **b)** 1743   **c)** 2168
6. **a) – b)** Check each number and word matches the beads drawn on each abacus.

Pages 8–9
1. **a)** <   **b)** >
   c) >   **d)** <
2. 1479, (1974)
3. **a)** 2087, 2900, 3149, 3150
   b) 5904, 5933, 6102, 6244
   c) 8003, 8030, 8300, 8303
   d) 8599, 8959, 9132, 9213
4. Everest – 8848 m; K2 – 8611 m; Lenin Peak – 7134 m; Aconcagua – 6960 m; McKinley – 6194 m; Kilimanjaro – 5893 m; Cook – 3766 m; Chappal Waddi – 2409 m

Pages 10–11
1. **a)** 82   **b)** 67
   c) 43   **d)** 93
   e) 71   **f)** 72
   g) 71   **h)** 87
2. **a)** 131   **b)** 114
   c) 115   **d)** 108
   e) 424   **f)** 317
   g) 261   **h)** 319
3. **a)**

+	80	60	90	70
253	333	313	343	323
185	265	245	275	255
693	773	753	783	763

b)

+	45	38	52	127
35	80	73	87	162
26	71	64	78	153
241	286	279	293	368

4. 45 + **3**8 = 83, **5**6 + 14 = **7**0, 19 + 4**4** = **6**3, 1**7** + 35 = 5**2**
5. 60

Pages 12–13
1. **a)** 37   **b)** 16
   c) 39   **d)** 47
   e) 29   **f)** 18
2. **a)** 95   **b)** 78
   c) 72   **d)** 71
   e) 78
3. **a)** Bottom row should be completed as follows: 93, 35, 62, 41, 79
   b) Bottom row should be completed as follows: 650, 150, 450, 550, 350
4. **a)** 45 cm   **b)** 35 cm
   c) 55 cm   **d)** 20 cm
   e) 30 cm

Page 14
1. −3, 7		2. 700, 30	
3. 300, 250		4. 1476	
5. 167, 162		6. 1596, 1956, 1965	
7. 2371		8. 410	
9. 3440, 3450		10. 5476, (7456)	
11. 230		12. 32, 44	
13. 982, 1082		14. 8915	
15. 8351		16. 6701	
17. −8, −5		18. 100, 104	
19. >, <		20. 4470	

Page 15
1. 80		2. 61	
3. 80		4. 323	
5. 618		6. 80	
7. 155		8. 56	
9. 250, 550		10. 33	
11. 53		12. 350 ml	
13. 86		14. 49	
15. 521, 237		16. 126	
17. 81		18. 57	
19. 99		20. 62	

Pages 16–17
1. **a)** 7 × 5 = 35, 5 × 7 = 35, 35 ÷ 5 = 7, 35 ÷ 7 = 5
   b) 6 × 7 = 42, 7 × 6 = 42, 42 ÷ 6 = 7, 42 ÷ 7 = 6
   c) 9 × 4 = 36, 4 × 9 = 36, 36 ÷ 9 = 4, 36 ÷ 4 = 9
   d) 8 × 6 = 48, 6 × 8 = 48, 48 ÷ 6 = 8, 48 ÷ 8 = 6
   e) 11 × 12 = 132, 12 × 11 = 132, 132 ÷ 11 = 12, 132 ÷ 12 = 11
   f) 7 × 9 = 63, 9 × 7 = 63, 63 ÷ 7 = 9, 63 ÷ 9 = 7

Answers

2. **a)** 54   **b)** 9
    c) 6   **d)** 9
    e) 7   **f)** 77
3. **a)** 9, 18, 36   **b)** 15, 30, 60
    c) 24, 48, 96   **d)** 12, 24, 48
    e) 27, 54, 108   **f)** 21, 42, 84
4. 88, 28, 27, 42
 72, 22, 36, 80
 21, 18, 18, 121
 60, 56, 81, 48
5. **a)** 56   **b)** 7   **c)** 21   **d)** 9

Pages 18–19

1. **a)** 36, 3600   **b)** 48, 4800
    c) 56, 5600   **d)** 27, 2700
    e) 49, 4900   **f)** 48, 4800
2.

×	30	60	80
20	600	1200	1600
90	2700	5400	7200
40	1200	2400	3200

3. **a)** 600   **b)** 9
    c) 2400   **d)** 500
    e) 2800   **f)** 300
4. **a)** 60   **b)** 240
    c) 120   **d)** 90
5. **a)** Factors of 25: 5, 5
    Factors of 4: 2, 2 $5 \times 5 \times 2 \times 2 = 100$
    b) Factors of 15: 3, 5
    Factors of 8: 2, 4 $3 \times 5 \times 2 \times 4 = 120$
    c) Factors of 35: 5, 7
    Factors of 6: 2, 3 $5 \times 7 \times 2 \times 3 = 210$
    d) Factors of 45: 5, 9
    Factors of 4: 2, 2 $5 \times 9 \times 2 \times 2 = 180$

Pages 20–21

1. **a)** 15   **b)** 17   **c)** 19
    d) 12   **e)** 13   **f)** 23
    g) 13   **h)** 28
2. no remainder → 84 ÷ 4
    1 → 61 ÷ 3
    2 → 74 ÷ 6
    3 → 78 ÷ 5
    4 → 92 ÷ 8
    5 → 86 ÷ 9
3. **a)** Bottom row should be completed as follows:
    500, 700, 400, 800, 900
    b) Bottom row should be completed as follows:
    600, 300, 800, 400, 700
4. **a)** 24   **b)** 18
    c) 14   **d)** 5 piles, 5 tyres left over

Pages 22–23

1. **a)** $\frac{3}{4}, \frac{6}{8}$ **b)** $\frac{2}{3}, \frac{6}{9}$
    c) $\frac{4}{5}, \frac{8}{10}$ **d)** $\frac{2}{5}, \frac{6}{15}$
2. Red $= \frac{2}{10}$ Yellow $= \frac{5}{10}$ Green $= \frac{3}{10}$
    $\frac{5}{10} > \frac{3}{10} > \frac{2}{10}$
3. Red $= \frac{1}{15}$ Yellow $= \frac{4}{15}$ Green $= \frac{8}{15}$ Blue $= \frac{2}{15}$
    $\frac{1}{15} < \frac{2}{15} < \frac{4}{15} < \frac{8}{15}$
4. **a)** $\frac{6}{10}, \frac{9}{15}, \frac{12}{20}, \frac{15}{25}, \frac{18}{30}$
    b) $\frac{6}{8}, \frac{9}{12}, \frac{12}{16}, \frac{15}{20}, \frac{18}{24}$
    c) $\frac{14}{20}, \frac{21}{30}, \frac{28}{40}, \frac{35}{50}, \frac{42}{60}$
    d) $\frac{6}{16}, \frac{9}{24}, \frac{12}{32}, \frac{15}{40}, \frac{18}{48}$

Pages 24–25

1. **a)** 18   **b)** 21
    c) 9   **d)** 12
2. **a)** 11, 22   **b)** 12, 36
    c) 7, 28   **d)** 6, 30
    e) 8, 56   **f)** 3, 15
3. $\frac{3}{5}$ of 40 = 24, $\frac{3}{4}$ of 40 = 30, $\frac{5}{8}$ of 40 = 25, so $\frac{3}{4}$ of 40
4. **a)** >   **b)** >
    c) <   **d)** >
    e) <   **f)** <
5. **a)** silver → 24   **b)** white → 10
    c) red → 18   **d)** black → 8

Pages 26–27

1. **a)** $\frac{4}{100}$, 0.04   **b)** $\frac{9}{100}$, 0.09
    c) $\frac{15}{100}$, 0.15   **d)** $\frac{2}{10}$, 0.2
    e) $\frac{22}{100}$, 0.22   **f)** $\frac{28}{100}$, 0.28
2. **a)** $\frac{2}{4}$ or $\frac{1}{2}$, or 0.5   **b)** $\frac{4}{6}$ or $\frac{2}{3}$, 0.66 (recurring)
    c) $\frac{11}{10}$ (or $1\frac{1}{10}$)   **d)** $\frac{7}{5}$ (or $1\frac{2}{5}$)
3. **a)** $\frac{2}{8}$ (or $\frac{1}{4}$)   **b)** $\frac{2}{10}$ (or $\frac{1}{5}$)
    c) $\frac{3}{5}$ **d)** $\frac{6}{10}$ (or $\frac{3}{5}$)
4.

$$\boxed{\frac{1}{5}}\ \boxed{\frac{3}{10}}\ \boxed{\frac{2}{5}}\ \boxed{\frac{1}{2}}\ \boxed{\frac{3}{5}}\ \boxed{\frac{7}{10}}\ \boxed{\frac{4}{5}}\ \boxed{\frac{9}{10}}$$

0   1

Page 28

1. 72   **2.** 36, 3600
3. 4   **4.** 84
5. 8   **6.** 240 g
7. 18   **8.** 1200
9. 4 packs, 8 balloons left over   **10.** 900
11. Factors of 14: 2, 7   Factors of 6: 2, 3
     $2 \times 7 \times 2 \times 3 = 84$

12. 4200

13. 18, 36, 72

14. 64

15. 7 r 3

16. 700

17. 3000

18. 96

19. 14

20. r = 1

Page 29

1. Any 8 parts shaded; any 4 parts shaded

2. <

3. $\boxed{\frac{9}{10}}$, $\frac{2}{10}$

4. 2

5. $\frac{2}{3}$, $\frac{4}{6}$

6. $\frac{16}{20}$

7. $\frac{4}{8}$ (or $\frac{1}{2}$ or $\frac{2}{4}$)

8.

9. $\frac{10}{12}$, $\frac{15}{18}$

10. $\frac{4}{10} < \frac{6}{10} < \frac{8}{10}$

11. $\frac{13}{100}$

12. $\frac{5}{10}$ or $\frac{1}{2}$

13. Any 5 parts blue; any 2 parts red

14. 5, 15

15. 10 pink, 8 blue and 42 white

16. $\frac{9}{18}$

17. $\frac{4}{5}$

18. $\frac{4}{5}$ of 40

19. $\frac{5}{10}$ (or $\frac{1}{2}$)

20. 0.39

Pages 30–31

1. **a)** 8 **b)** 91
   c) 356 **d)** 4.2
   e) 0.7 **f)** 83.5

2. **a)** 9.6 **b)** 0.8
   c) 14.3 **d)** 0.52
   e) 0.04 **f)** 0.706

3. **a)** 194 **b)** 520
   c) 3495 **d)** 60
   e) 2 **f)** 4705

4. **a)** 6.74 **b)** 28.9
   c) 0.71 **d)** 0.352
   e) 0.109 **f)** 0.4

5. **a)** × 10 **b)** ÷ 100
   c) × 100 **d)** ÷ 100
   e) × 10 **f)** ÷ 100

Pages 32–33

1. **a)** 3.5, 5.3, 5.6, 6.3, 6.5
   b) 11.6, 11.8, 12.1, 12.3, 12.5
   c) 22.7, 22.9, 23.1, 23.6, 23.8
   d) 0.25, 0.55, 0.81, 0.85, 0.92
   e) 2.95, 3.17, 3.22, 3.25, 3.27
   f) 8.51, 8.54, 9.06, 9.09, 9.56

2. **a)** 3 **b)** 4
   c) 4 **d)** 5
   e) 6 **f)** 6

3. **a)** 1 **b)** 8
   c) 3 **d)** 20
   e) 35 **f)** 26

4. Gold medal – 7.13 m; Silver medal – 7.05 m;
   Bronze medal – 7.04 m; 4th place – 6.91 m;
   5th place – 6.85 m; 6th place – 6.83 m

Pages 34–35

1. **a)** 1.1 **b)** 1.3
   c) 1.4 **d)** 1.4
   e) 1.4 **f)** 1.5

2. **a)** 1.4 **b)** 0.7
   c) 1.4 **d)** 0.5
   e) 0.8 **f)** 0.8

3. **a)** 1.2 **b)** 0.4
   c) 0.8 **d)** 1.4
   e) 0.6 **f)** 0.2
   g) 1.8 **h)** 1.6

4. **a)** **1.4** – 0.7 = 0.7
   b) **1.2** – 0.8 = 0.4
   c) £1.**05** + £1.32 = £2.37
   d) £2.2**3** + £3.41 = £**5**.64

Pages 36–37

1. **a)** 0.55 m **b)** 3500 g
   c) 3500 ml **d)** 128 cm
   e) 4 l 200 ml **f)** 2 kg 450 g
   g) 8000 m **h)** 7 cm 5 mm
   i) 3.2 m **j)** 2 km

2. **a)** > **b)** =
   c) > **d)** <
   e) = **f)** <
   g) > **h)** >

3. **a)** 5 m **b)** 3 kg
   c) 6 litres **d)** 17 km
   e) 64 kg **f)** 5 m

4. 4

Pages 38–39

1. **a)** £1.84 **b)** £2.52
   c) £1.80 **d)** £2.37

2. **a)** £4.60 **b)** £1.70
   c) £3.90 **d)** £4.80
   e) £1.10 **f)** £1.50

3. **a)** 20p **b)** 70p
   c) 5p **d)** 25p
   e) £1.10 **f)** 95p

Answers

4.

Ice-lollies

		0	1	2	3	4
Ice-creams	**0**	0	20p	40p	60p	**80p**
	1	50p	70p	**90p**	£1.10	£1.30
	2	£1.00	£1.20	**£1.40**	**£1.60**	**£1.80**
	3	£1.50	**£1.70**	**£1.90**	£2.10	£2.30
	4	**£2.00**	**£2.20**	**£2.40**	**£2.60**	**£2.80**

3 ice-creams; 4 ice-lollies

Pages 40–41
1. a) 2.45   b) 10.05
   c) 6.40   d) 8.33
   e) 1.17   f) 9.59
   g) 11.03   h) 6.21
2. a) afternoon   b) morning
   c) morning   d) evening
   e) afternoon   f) evening
3. a) 19:28   b) 05:17
   c) 23:52
4. a) 6.35 a.m.   b) 12.07 p.m.
   c) 10.10 p.m.
5. a) 5 minutes   b) 28 days
   c) 150 seconds   d) 270 minutes
   e) 42 months   f) 8 weeks
   g) 10 days   h) 2 hours
   i) 1800 seconds j) 168 hours

Page 42
1. 4.6 < 6.4 < 6.7 < 7.4 < 7.6   2. 19
3. 0.54   4. 1.25
5. × 100, × 10   6. 14, 1.4
7. 0.318   8. 5, 11
9. 4   10. 1.3, 0.7
11. 6710   12. 13.2
13. 1.1   14. 1.38 < 1.83 < 3.18 < 8.13 < 8.31
15. 0.45   16. 1.6
17. 10, 12   18. ÷, ×
19. 50.7   20. ÷ 10, ÷ 100

Page 43
1. 4 kg 810 g   2. 850 mm
3. 5 kg   4. 1600 ml
5. 9.26 a.m., 3.55 p.m. 6. 7000 m
7. 30p   8. 180 minutes
9. 1530 cm   10. <, =
11. £2.90   12. 3 m
13. 3.45 p.m.   14. 7500 g
15. morning   16. £4.25
17. 24 l, 1 km   18. 48 hours
19. 11.46 a.m.   20. £1.75

2 This circle is divided into tenths. Write the fraction for each colour.

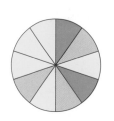

Red = $\dfrac{\Box}{10}$ Yellow = $\dfrac{\Box}{10}$ Green = $\dfrac{\Box}{10}$

Now write the fractions in order starting with the largest.

3 This rectangle is divided into 15 parts. Write a fraction for each colour.

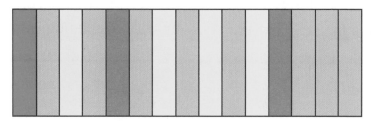

Red = $\dfrac{\Box}{15}$ Yellow = $\dfrac{\Box}{15}$ Green = $\dfrac{\Box}{15}$ Blue = $\dfrac{\Box}{15}$

Now write the fractions in order starting with the smallest.

Challenge yourself

4 Copy and complete each of these successive equivalent fractions.

a) $\dfrac{3}{5} = \dfrac{6}{\Box} = \dfrac{\Box}{15} = \dfrac{12}{\Box} = \dfrac{\Box}{\Box} = \dfrac{\Box}{\Box}$

b) $\dfrac{3}{4} = \dfrac{\Box}{8} = \dfrac{9}{\Box} = \dfrac{\Box}{16} = \dfrac{\Box}{\Box} = \dfrac{\Box}{\Box}$

c) $\dfrac{7}{10} = \dfrac{14}{\Box} = \dfrac{\Box}{30} = \dfrac{28}{\Box} = \dfrac{\Box}{\Box} = \dfrac{\Box}{\Box}$

d) $\dfrac{3}{8} = \dfrac{\Box}{16} = \dfrac{9}{\Box} = \dfrac{\Box}{32} = \dfrac{\Box}{\Box} = \dfrac{\Box}{\Box}$

How did you do?

23

Fractions of amounts

When you need to find fractions of amounts, use the numerator and denominator.

Example: What is $\frac{1}{5}$ of 20?

When the numerator is 1, just divide by the denominator.

$$\frac{1}{5} \text{ of } 20 = 20 \div 5 = 4$$

Example: What is $\frac{3}{5}$ of 20?

When the numerator is more than 1, divide by the denominator then multiply by the numerator.

$$\frac{1}{5} \text{ of } 20 = 4$$

$\frac{3}{5}$ is the same as $\frac{1}{5} \times 3$

$$\left(\frac{1}{5} + \frac{1}{5} + \frac{1}{5}\right)$$

So $\frac{3}{5}$ of 20 = 4 × 3 = 12

Warm up

1 Work out three-quarters of each group of trees.

a) $\frac{3}{4}$ of 24 =

b) 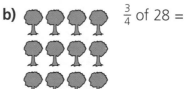 $\frac{3}{4}$ of 28 =

c)  $\frac{3}{4}$ of 12 =

d) $\frac{3}{4}$ of 16 =

2 Answer each pair of questions.

a) $\frac{1}{3}$ of 33 =

$\frac{2}{3}$ of 33 =

b) $\frac{1}{4}$ of 48 =

$\frac{3}{4}$ of 48 =

c) $\frac{1}{5}$ of 35 =

$\frac{4}{5}$ of 35 =

d) $\frac{1}{6}$ of 36 =

$\frac{5}{6}$ of 36 =

e) $\frac{1}{10}$ of 80 =

$\frac{7}{10}$ of 80 =

f) $\frac{1}{8}$ of 24 =

$\frac{5}{8}$ of 24 =

3 Here are 40 flowers.

Which would give you the greatest number of flowers, $\frac{3}{5}$, $\frac{3}{4}$ or $\frac{5}{8}$ of them? Choose the correct answer.

a) $\frac{3}{5}$ of 40

b) $\frac{3}{4}$ of 40

c) $\frac{5}{8}$ of 40

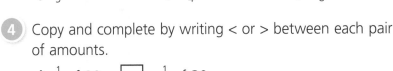

4 Copy and complete by writing < or > between each pair of amounts.

a) $\frac{1}{3}$ of 30 ☐ $\frac{1}{5}$ of 30

b) $\frac{1}{4}$ of 20 ☐ $\frac{1}{5}$ of 20

c) $\frac{1}{10}$ of 50 ☐ $\frac{1}{5}$ of 50

d) $\frac{1}{8}$ of 40 ☐ $\frac{1}{10}$ of 40

e) $\frac{1}{10}$ of 60 ☐ $\frac{1}{3}$ of 60

f) $\frac{1}{5}$ of 100 ☐ $\frac{1}{4}$ of 100

5 In a car park there are 60 cars. How many of each colour are there?

a) $\frac{2}{5}$ are silver =

b) $\frac{1}{6}$ are white =

c) $\frac{3}{10}$ are red =

d) $\frac{2}{15}$ are black =

How did you do?

Fraction problems

Fractions can be shown on a number line.

This number line is divided into tenths and hundredths. They are written as common fractions $\left(\text{e.g. } \frac{1}{100}\right)$ and as decimal fractions (e.g. 0.01).

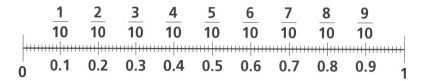

| $\frac{1}{10}$ | $\frac{2}{10}$ | $\frac{3}{10}$ | $\frac{4}{10}$ | $\frac{5}{10}$ | $\frac{6}{10}$ | $\frac{7}{10}$ | $\frac{8}{10}$ | $\frac{9}{10}$ |

0   0.1   0.2   0.3   0.4   0.5   0.6   0.7   0.8   0.9   1

If we zoom into the numbers between 0 and $\frac{1}{10}$, we can count in hundredths.

0   $\frac{1}{100}$ $\frac{2}{100}$ $\frac{3}{100}$ $\frac{4}{100}$ $\frac{5}{100}$ $\frac{6}{100}$ $\frac{7}{100}$ $\frac{8}{100}$ $\frac{9}{100}$ $\frac{10}{100}$

0   0.01   0.02   0.03   0.04   0.05   0.06   0.07   0.08   0.09   0.1

$\frac{1}{100}$ = 0.01   zero point zero one

$\frac{2}{100}$ = 0.02   zero point zero two

Warm up

1 Write both the common fraction and decimal fraction for each arrow.

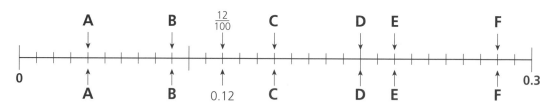

It is easy to add and subtract fractions with the same denominator – just add or subtract the numerators. For example:

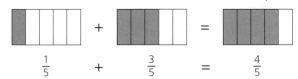

$$\frac{1}{5} \quad + \quad \frac{3}{5} \quad = \quad \frac{4}{5}$$

2 Add these fractions. Give your answer as a fraction and a decimal in parts **a** and **b**. Use the images to help you.

a)

$\frac{1}{4} + \frac{1}{4} = \dfrac{\square}{\square}$ or _____

b)

$\frac{2}{6} + \frac{2}{6} = \dfrac{\square}{\square}$ or _____

c)

$\frac{6}{10} + \frac{5}{10} = \dfrac{\square}{\square}$

d)

$\frac{3}{5} + \frac{4}{5} = \dfrac{\square}{\square}$

3 Subtract these fractions.

a) $\frac{5}{8} - \frac{3}{8} =$ 　　　　　　**b)** $\frac{3}{10} - \frac{1}{10} =$

c) $\frac{4}{5} - \frac{1}{5} =$ 　　　　　　**d)** $\frac{9}{10} - \frac{3}{10} =$

4 Copy this number line and write each of these fractions in the correct position.

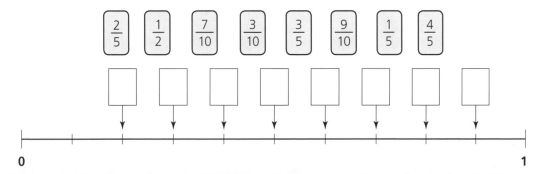

$\boxed{\frac{2}{5}}$ $\boxed{\frac{1}{2}}$ $\boxed{\frac{7}{10}}$ $\boxed{\frac{3}{10}}$ $\boxed{\frac{3}{5}}$ $\boxed{\frac{9}{10}}$ $\boxed{\frac{1}{5}}$ $\boxed{\frac{4}{5}}$

0　　　　　　　　　　　　　　　　　1

How did you do?

Progress test 3

1. $8 \times 9 =$

2. Answer both of these multiplications.

   $9 \times 4 \quad =$

   $9 \times 400 =$

3. $11 \times \underline{\hspace{2cm}} = 44$

4. $12 \times 7 =$

5. $56 \div 7 =$

6. What is the total weight of three cakes weighing 80 g each?

7. $90 \div 5 =$

8. $40 \times 30 =$

9. 40 balloons are needed for a party and there are 12 balloons in a pack.
   How many packs of balloons will be needed, and how many balloons will be left over?

10. $3600 \div 4 =$

11. Use factors to help multiply 14 by 6.

    Factors of 14: \underline{\hspace{1.5cm}} \underline{\hspace{1.5cm}}

    Factors of 6: \underline{\hspace{1.5cm}} \underline{\hspace{1.5cm}}

    \underline{\hspace{1cm}} $\times$ \underline{\hspace{1cm}} $\times$ \underline{\hspace{1cm}} $\times$ \underline{\hspace{1cm}} $=$ \underline{\hspace{1cm}}

12. $6 \times 700 =$

13. Answer these multiplications.

    $6 \times 3 \quad =$

    $6 \times 6 \quad =$

    $6 \times 12 =$

14. $4 \times 8 \times 2 =$

15. Answer this division. Give the remainder.

    $45 \div 6 =$ \underline{\hspace{2cm}} r \underline{\hspace{1.5cm}}

16. What is 3500 divided by 5?

17. $50 \times 60 =$

18. $8 \times 12 =$

19. $84 \div 6 =$

20. What is the remainder when 28 is divided by 3?

Score ◯ / 20

1 Copy the rectangles and colour $\frac{2}{3}$ of each.

2 Write < or > in between these fractions to make this true.

$\frac{1}{10}$ of 20 ☐ $\frac{1}{5}$ of 20

3 Copy these fractions. Circle the largest fraction and underline the smallest fraction.

$\frac{7}{10}$ $\frac{2}{10}$ $\frac{9}{10}$ $\frac{5}{10}$ $\frac{3}{10}$

4 A box has 12 eggs. $\frac{1}{6}$ of the eggs are broken. How many eggs are broken?

5 Write the pair of equivalent fractions for each part shaded blue.

6 Write the next equivalent fraction.

$\frac{4}{5} = \frac{8}{10} = \frac{12}{15} = \frac{☐}{☐}$

7 $\frac{7}{8} - \frac{3}{8} =$

8 Copy this number line and write $\frac{3}{10}$ and $\frac{4}{5}$ in the correct positions on it.

0 ———————————— 1

9 Write the missing numbers in this equivalent fractions chain.

$\frac{5}{6} = \frac{☐}{12} = \frac{15}{☐}$

10 Write these in order, smallest first.

$\frac{4}{10}$ $\frac{8}{10}$ $\frac{6}{10}$

11 This arrow is at 0.13. Which is the matching common fraction?

0   0.1   0.2

$\frac{3}{10}$ $\frac{1}{3}$ $\frac{13}{100}$ $\frac{30}{100}$

12 $\frac{4}{10} + \frac{1}{10} =$ _____ or _____

13 Copy this rectangle. Shade $\frac{5}{8}$ of it blue and $\frac{1}{4}$ red.

14 Answer these.

$\frac{1}{8}$ of 40 = $\frac{3}{8}$ of 40 =

15 There are 60 flowers in a vase. Write how many of each colour.

$\frac{1}{6}$ pink   =

$\frac{2}{15}$ blue   =

$\frac{7}{10}$ white =

16 Which fraction is equivalent to $\frac{3}{6}$?

$\frac{6}{9}$ $\frac{9}{18}$ $\frac{12}{18}$

17 $\frac{2}{5} + \frac{2}{5} =$

18 Which is the greatest amount?

$\frac{3}{4}$ of 40 $\frac{7}{10}$ of 40 $\frac{4}{5}$ of 40

19 $\frac{9}{10} - \frac{4}{10} = \frac{☐}{☐}$

20 Which decimal fraction below matches $\frac{39}{100}$?

0.39   0.039   3.9   3.09

Score ⬤/20

Decimals

Follow these rules for multiplying and dividing numbers by 10 and 100.

To multiply by 10

Move the digits **one** place to the **left**.

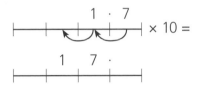

To multiply by 100

Move the digits **two** places to the **left**.

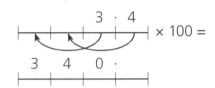

To divide by 10

Move the digits **one** place to the **right**.

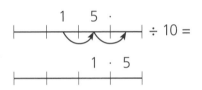

To divide by 100

Move the digits **two** places to the **right**.

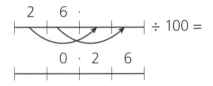

Fill any spaces with zeros. Putting a zero on the end of a decimal does not change the number.

For example, 1.2 is the same as 1.20 and 1.200

Warm up

1 Multiply these by 10 and write the answers.

    a) $0.8 \times 10 =$ **b)** $9.1 \times 10 =$

    c) $35.6 \times 10 =$ **d)** $0.42 \times 10 =$

    e) $0.07 \times 10 =$ **f)** $8.35 \times 10 =$

2 Divide these by 10 and write the answers.

    a) $96 \div 10 =$ **b)** $8 \div 10 =$

    c) $143 \div 10 =$ **d)** $5.2 \div 10 =$

    e) $0.4 \div 10 =$ **f)** $7.06 \div 10 =$

3 Multiply these by 100 and write the answers.

a) 1.94 × 100 =

b) 5.2 × 100 =

c) 34.95 × 100 =

d) 0.6 × 100 =

e) 0.02 × 100 =

f) 47.05 × 100 =

4 Divide these by 100 and write the answers.

a) 674 ÷ 100 =

b) 2890 ÷ 100 =

c) 71 ÷ 100 =

d) 35.2 ÷ 100 =

e) 10.9 ÷ 100 =

f) 40 ÷ 100 =

Challenge yourself

5 Write the missing operation for each of these. Is it **× 10**, **× 100**, **÷ 10** or **÷ 100**?

a) 1.5 — 15

b) 29 — 0.29

c) 6.29 — 629

d) 580 — 5.8

e) 74.3 — 743

f) 8 — 0.08

How did you do?

31

Ordering and rounding decimals

When you compare and order tenths or hundredths, look carefully at the value of each digit.

Example: Put these in order, starting with the smallest.

3.4   3.8   2.9   4.3

Look at the whole numbers and then the tenths. The order is:

2.9   3.4   3.8   4.3

Example: Put these in order, starting with the smallest.

1.65   1.05   1.68   0.65

Look at the whole numbers, then the tenths, then the hundredths. The order is:

0.65   1.05   1.65   1.68

Decimal numbers can be rounded to the nearest whole number.

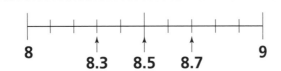

When rounding decimals look at the tenths digit:

- If it is 5 or more, round up to the next whole number.
- If it is less than 5, round down and the whole number stays the same.

8.<u>7</u> rounds up to 9

8.<u>3</u> rounds down to 8

8.<u>5</u> rounds up to 9

Warm up

1 Write each set of numbers in order, starting with the smallest.

a)
| 5.6 | | 5.3 | | 3.5 |
| | 6.3 | | 6.5 | |

b)
| 11.8 | | 11.6 | | 12.3 |
| | 12.5 | | 12.1 | |

c)
| 23.6 | | 22.9 | | 22.7 |
| | 23.1 | | 23.8 | |

d)

0.85	0.92	0.55
0.81	0.25	

e)

3.27	3.25	3.17
3.22	2.95	

f)

9.06	8.54	9.09
9.56	8.51	

2 Round each decimal number to the nearest whole number.
Use the number line to help you.

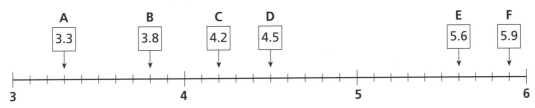

3 Round each of these to the nearest whole number.

a) 1.3 **b)** 7.8 **c)** 2.5

d) 20.1 **e)** 34.6 **f)** 25.7

4 These are the lengths in metres jumped by six long-jump athletes.
Write the lengths in order starting with the longest.

Gold medal	m
Silver medal	m
Bronze medal	m
4th place	m
5th place	m
6th place	m

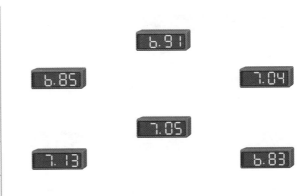

How did you do?

Decimal calculations

Here are two ways to help you add tenths.
These both show that 0.8 + 0.5 = 1.3.

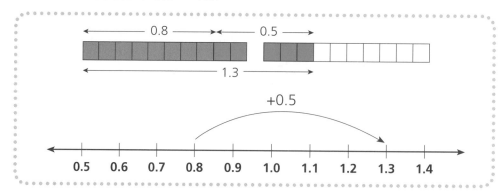

Use facts you know to calculate with decimals.

8 + 5 = 13

0.8 + 0.5 = 1.3

13 − 8 = 5

1.3 − 0.8 = 0.5

Warm up

1 Each whole rod is divided into tenths. Use them to help work out these decimal additions.

a)

0.5 + 0.6 =

b)

0.9 + 0.4 =

c)

0.7 + 0.7 =

d)

0.6 + 0.8 =

e)

0.5 + 0.9 =

f)

0.8 + 0.7 =

2 Use the number lines to help you answer these subtractions.

a)
0.2   2.0

1.8 – 0.4 =

b)
0.6   1.7

1.5 – 0.8 =

c)
0.3   2.1

1.9 – 0.5 =

d)
0.5   1.4

1.2 – 0.7 =

e)
0.7   1.9

1.7 – 0.9 =

f)
0.4   1.6

1.4 – 0.6 =

3 Use the number line to help you answer these calculations.

0   0.2   0.4   0.6   0.8   1   1.2   1.4   1.6   1.8   2

a) 0.8 + 0.4   b) 1.6 – 1.2

c) 1.3 – 0.5   d) 0.6 + 0.8

e) 1.5 – 0.9   f) 1.7 – 1.5

g) 0.9 + 0.9   h) 1.2 + 0.4

4 Write the missing digits 0–5 for each calculation.

0   **2**   **4**

1   **3**   **5**

a) 1.⬚ – 0.7 = 0.7   b) ⬚.⬚ – 0.8 = 0.4

c) £1.⬚5 + £1.32 = £2.37   d) £2.2⬚ + £3.41 = £⬚.64

How did you do?

Measures

Length

You measure the length of objects in millimetres (mm), centimetres (cm), metres (m) and kilometres (km).

10 mm = 1 cm
100 cm = 1 m
1000 m = 1 km

Capacity

You measure the capacity of containers in millilitres (ml) and litres (l).

1000 ml = 1 litres

Mass

You measure the mass or weight of an object in grams (g) and kilograms (kg).

1000 g = 1 kg

You may often use decimals when measuring. For example, you can measure lengths using a mixture of centimetres and metres.

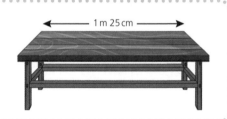

This table is 1 metre 25 centimetres long.

1 m 25 cm = 1.25 m = 125 cm

The decimal point separates the centimetres from the metres.

Lengths under 1 m can still be written as decimals, e.g. 32 cm is written as 0.32 m.

Warm up

1 Write the equivalent measures.

a) 55 cm = _____ m

b) $3\frac{1}{2}$ kg = _____ g

c) 3.5 l = _____ ml

d) 1.28 m = _____ cm

e) 4200 ml = _____ litres _____ ml

f) 2450 g = _____ kg _____ g

g) 8 km = _____ m

h) 75 mm = _____ cm _____ mm

i) 320 cm = _____ m

j) 2000 m = _____ km

2 Copy and write < , > or = in between the measurements to make each of these true.

a) 1.86 m ☐ 1 m 68 cm

b) 1 m 10 cm ☐ 110 cm

c) 472 cm ☐ 2.74 m

d) 3 m 9 cm ☐ 3.9 m

e) 835 cm ☐ 8 m 35 cm

f) 1.06 m ☐ 160 cm

g) 5.81 m ☐ 1 m 85 cm

h) 46 cm ☐ 0.42 m

3 Work out the missing measurements, changing each decimal to the nearest whole number.

a)
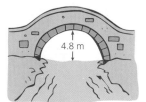
4.8 m

This bridge is approximately _____ m high.

b)

FLOUR
3.4 kg

This sack of flour weighs approximately _____ kg.

c)

5.5 litres

This bucket holds approximately _____ litres of water.

d)

Leeds
17.2 km

It is approximately _____ km to Leeds.

e)

63 kg   64 kg   65 kg

This woman weighs approximately _____ kg.

f)
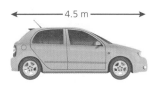
4.5 m

This car is approximately _____ m long.

4 James uses a 3.5-litre jug and a 2.5-litre jug to fill a fish tank that holds 19 litres. He works out that he can use a mixture of full jugs to make the exact total of 19 litres.

If James uses two 2.5-litre jugs, how many 3.5-litre jugs will he need to fill the tank?

How did you do?

Money

Look at these coins.

There are 100 pence in £1.

£1 = 100p

We use a decimal point to separate pounds and pence:

£1.25 = 125p or £1 and 25p   £2.30 = 230p or £2 and 30p

Warm up

1 How much money is in each purse?

a)

b)

c)

d)

Test yourself

2 Find the total of each pair of prices.

a) £3.50 £1.10

b) £0.40 £1.30

c) £1.70 £2.20

d) £1.10 £3.70

e) £0.60 £0.50

f) £0.80 £0.70

3 Write the change from £2 for each of these.

a)   £1.80

b)   £1.30

c)   £1.95

d) £1.75

e)   £0.90

f) £1.05

Challenge yourself

4 Ice-creams cost 50p each and ice-lollies cost 20p each.
Amir buys some for his friends.

a) Copy and complete this chart to show the cost of buying different amounts.
Look for patterns in the totals.

Ice-lollies

		0	1	2	3	4
Ice-creams	0	0	20p	40p	60p	
	1	50p	70p			
	2	£1.00	£1.20			
	3	£1.50				
	4					

b) If Amir spends £2.30 in total, how many of each does he buy?

How did you do?

Time

There are 60 minutes in one hour.

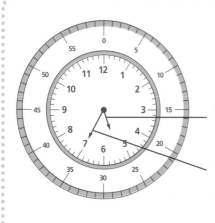

05.35

This shows the hour. It is past 5 o'clock.

This shows the number of minutes past the hour. It is 35 minutes past 5 or 5.35.

This clock shows 37 minutes past 5, or 5.37.

To read this, count on two more minutes past 5.35.

a.m. (ante meridiem) means before midday, so morning times.

p.m. (post meridiem) means after midday, so afternoon and evening times.

Warm up

1 Write the times shown on each clock face.

a)
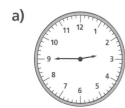

b)

c)

d)

e)
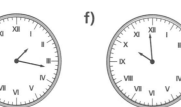

f)

g)
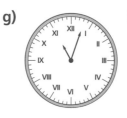

h)
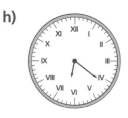

2 Are these times morning times **or** afternoon/evening times?

a) 2.07 p.m.   b) 7.18 a.m.   c) 9.12 a.m.

d) 8.26 p.m.   e) 3.54 p.m.   f) 9.04 p.m.

3 Write these times using the 24-hour digital clock.

a) 7.28 p.m.

b) 5.17 a.m.

c) 11.52 p.m.

4 Write these times using the 12-hour clock, remembering to use a.m. or p.m. in your answer.

a) 06:35

b) 12:07

c) 22:10

Challenge yourself

5 Copy and complete these.

a) 300 seconds = _____ minutes   b) 4 weeks = _____ days

c) $2\frac{1}{2}$ minutes = _____ seconds   d) $4\frac{1}{2}$ hours = _____ minutes

e) $3\frac{1}{2}$ years = _____ months   f) 56 days = _____ weeks

g) 240 hours = _____ days   h) 120 minutes = _____ hours

i) $\frac{1}{2}$ hour = _____ seconds   j) 1 week = _____ hours

How did you do?

Progress test 5

1 Write these in order smallest first.

6.4 4.6 7.4 7.6 6.7

2 $1.9 \times 10 =$

3 $5.4 \div 10 =$

4 Which is the smallest decimal number?

5 Copy and complete these. Write **10** or **100** in the spaces.

$0.2 \times \underline{\hspace{1.5cm}} = 20$

$49.1 \times \underline{\hspace{1.5cm}} = 491$

6 Answer these calculations.

$9 + 5 =$

$0.9 + 0.5 =$

7 $3.18 \div 10 =$

8 Round to the nearest whole number.

5.3

10.6

9 $0.04 \times 100 =$

10 Use the number line to help you answer these.

$$\begin{array}{ccc} 0 & 1 & 2 \end{array}$$

$0.7 + 0.6 =$

$1.5 - 0.8 =$

11 $67.1 \times 100 =$

12 $132 \div 10 =$

13 $1.7 - 0.6 =$

14 Write these in order smallest first.

8.13 1.83 3.18 8.31 1.38

15 $45 \div 100 =$

16 $0.9 + 0.7 =$

17 Round to the nearest whole number.

9.5

12.4

18 Copy and complete these. Write **×** or **÷** in each.

$8.7 \boxed{} 10 = 0.87$

$8.7 \boxed{} 10 = 87$

19 $5.07 \times 10 =$

20 Copy and complete these. Write **10** or **100** in the spaces.

$94 \div \underline{\hspace{1.5cm}} = 9.4$

$37 \div \underline{\hspace{1.5cm}} = 0.37$

Score   ◯ / 20

1 4810 g = _____ kg _____ g

2 85 cm = _____ mm

3 What is 5.4 kg rounded to the nearest whole number?

4 1.6 litres = _____ ml

5 Write the time shown on each clock.

_____ a.m.   _____ p.m.

6 7 km = _____ m

7 An adult ticket costs £1.80 and a child's ticket is 90p. How much change will you get from £3 if you buy one adult ticket and one child's ticket?

8 3 hours = _____ minutes

9 15.3 m = _____ cm

10 Copy and complete these. Write <, > or = between the measurements to make them true.

142 cm ☐ 14 m

180 mm ☐ 18 cm

11 Write the total amount.

12 300 cm = _____ m

13 What is the time 1 hour 15 minutes later than 2.30 p.m.?

14 $7\frac{1}{2}$ kg = _____ g

15 When is 6.15 a.m.? Write the answer: **morning**, **afternoon** or **evening**.

16 What is the total of 80p and £3.45?

17 Round these to the nearest whole number.

24.3 litres

0.7 km

18 2 days = _____ hours

19 Sam's dentist appointment is at 11.36 a.m. He is 10 minutes late. What time does he arrive?

20 What change will be given from £5 if you spend £3.25?

Score ◯ / 20   43

Published by Keen Kite Books
An imprint of HarperCollins*Publishers* Ltd
The News Building
1 London Bridge Street
London SE1 9GF

ISBN 9780008161231

Text © 2013 Paul Broadbent and © 2015 Keen Kite
Books, an imprint of HarperCollins*Publishers* Ltd

Design © 2015 Keen Kite Books,
an imprint of HarperCollins*Publishers* Ltd